KU-126-011

CARS

James Nixon

FRANKLIN WATTS

LONDON • SYDNEY

 An Appleseed Editions book

First published in 2010 by Franklin Watts
338 Euston Road, London NW1 3BH

Franklin Watts Australia
Hachette Children's Books
Level 17/207 Kent St, Sydney, NSW 2000

© 2010 Appleseed Editions

Created by Appleseed Editions Ltd,
Well House, Friars Hill, Guestling,
East Sussex TN35 4ET

Planning and production by Discovery Books Limited
Designed by D.R. ink
Cover design by Blink Media
Edited by James Nixon

All rights reserved. No part of this publication may be reproduced,
stored in a retrieval system or transmitted in any form or by any means,
electronic, mechanical, photocopying, recording or otherwise, without
prior permission of the publisher.

ISBN 978 1 4451 0026 5

Dewey Classification: 629.2'22

A CIP catalogue for this book is available from the British Library.

Photograph acknowledgements
Alamy Images: p. 26 (Rich Edwards/ARPS); Bugatti Automobiles S.A.S: p. 5 top; Citroen
Communication: p. 8 bottom (S. Foulon); Corbis: pp. 7 top (Schlegelmilch), 18 (David Freers), 24 (Alan Look),
28 (Chris Williams/Icon SMI); General Motors: p. 19 bottom; Getty Images: p. 9 bottom (Hulton Archive), 12
(Scott Barbour), 15 (Drew Hallowell), 16 (Bertrand Guay/AFP), 17 (Paul Crook/AFP), 23 (Jeff J. Mitchell); Honda
Motor Europe Ltd: p. 6; Istockphoto.com: pp. 4, 19 top (Christy Seely); Lamborghini: p. 11 bottom; Museum of
British Road Transport: p. 29 bottom; Pagani Communciation: p. 13 bottom; Porsche: p. 10; Shelby Supercars:
p. 13 top; Shutterstock: pp. 5, 7 bottom (George Dolgikh), 8 top (Eky Chan), 8 middle, 11 top, 14 top (Digitalsport-
photoagency), 16 bottom (Max Earey), 20 (Nikos Douzinas), 21 (Elemer Sagi), 22, 27 top (Peter Weber), 27 bottom,
29 top (Juery Schreiter); Wikimedia: p. 25 top (Flickr).

Cover photos:

Printed in China

Franklin Watts is a division of Hachette Children's Books,
www.hachette.co.uk

DUDLEY PUBLIC LIBRARIES

L

748569   Bd

J629.22

DUDLEY SCHOOLS
LIBRARY SERVICE

Schools Library and Information Services

S0000748569

Contents

Cars everywhere

We use cars to travel on the roads from place to place. Cars come in many types, shapes and sizes. But they all work in the same way and have similar parts.

Fuel tank: This is at the back of the car. It is filled with a fuel, such as petrol, **diesel**, gas or **biofuel**.

Bonnet

Wheels

Speed king

Some roadcars go super speeds. The Bugatti Veyron can reach 254 mph (408 kph). It is the most expensive car in the world.

Engine: A car's engine is usually under the bonnet. Inside the engine, fuel is mixed with air and burned to produce energy. This provides the power to turn the car's wheels.

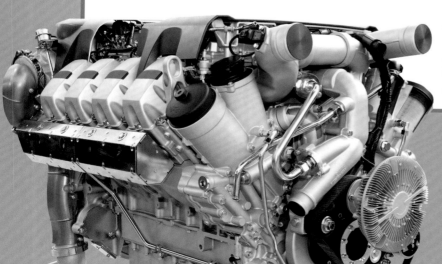

Behind the wheel

The driver has all sorts of controls for the car. There are levers to flick, pedals to push and buttons on the dashboard.

Displays on the dashboard tell the driver what speed the car is doing and how much fuel is left in the tank.

Steering wheel: turns the wheels

Indicator: flashes a light to show other cars which way the driver will turn

Accelerator: increases the car's speed

Brake: slows the car down

In the hotseat

The insides of some racing cars are tiny. The main controls are all on the steering wheel.

Gears: Most cars have at least five gears. The driver changes gear using the gearstick. Gears change the amount of power going to the car's wheels. If you are driving fast you need a high gear.

Family cars

Family cars are the most common cars on the roads. They usually have two rows of seats and a boot for carrying luggage or shopping.

There are different types of family car. A **saloon** has a different shaped rear end from a **hatchback**. People carriers have extra rows of seats.

Saloon

People carrier

Hatchback

Radiator

A running car engine gets hot. Cool water is passed through the engine to stop it overheating. The heated water is then passed into the **radiator**, behind the grill (right). Here the water can lose its heat into the air.

Grill

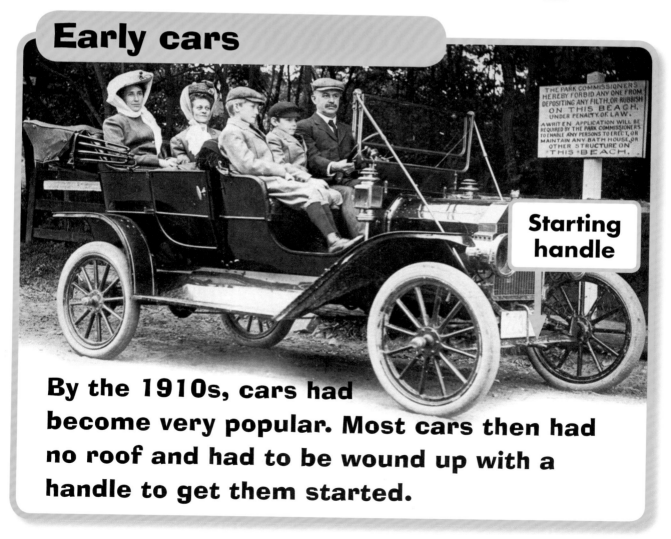

Early cars

Starting handle

By the 1910s, cars had become very popular. Most cars then had no roof and had to be wound up with a handle to get them started.

Sports cars

Drivers of sports cars are not worried about space and comfort. They want a car that looks good and is fun to drive.

Sports cars are fast and handle corners with ease. Many sports cars are **convertibles**. This means the roof can be folded away.

Carbon fibre parts

Sports cars are fast because they are very light. Bodywork parts are made out of a super-light material called **carbon fibre**. The threads in carbon fibre are really thin, but very strong, too.

Police cars

Police forces in some countries make use of speedy sports cars. In an emergency the Italian police use a Lamborghini Gallardo.

Supercars

Supercars are the fastest and most powerful cars on the road. You have to be very rich to own one of these.

Fast starter

The Koenigsegg **CCR** can get from a standing start to 60 mph (100 kph) in just three seconds!

Supercars are expensive because of their design. Some are very rare. The SSC Ultimate Aero (below) is the fastest roadcar in the world, but only 25 models will ever be built.

Exhaust

When fuel burns in an engine, gases are given off. A car's exhaust pipe lets these gases escape into the air. The Pagani Zonda's engine is so powerful that it needs four exhaust pipes.

Exhaust pipes

On the track

Motor racing is a popular and exciting sport. In touring car racing, ordinary roadcars are raced around motor circuits. Parts, such as the engine, brakes and tyres are changed to make the cars faster.

Roll cage

Touring cars have a frame built in or around the **cabin**. This strengthens the car and protects the driver if a car smashes or rolls over.

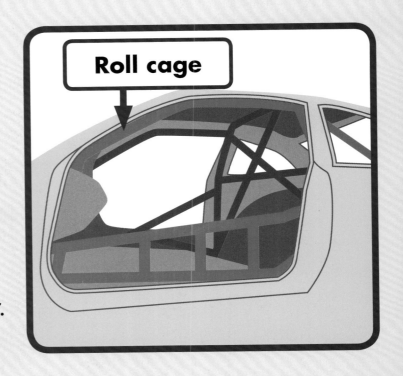

Roll cage

Stock car racing in the USA is similar to touring cars. The cars race around an oval track with banked sides. Huge crowds roar them on.

Crashing

Big crashes are common in high-speed motor racing, especially in stock car racing where the cars run so close together. To keep safe, drivers wear fireproof clothing and have special seatbelts and harnesses.

High-speed racing

Formula 1 (F1) racing is fast and noisy. These single-seater cars reach speeds of 220 mph (360 kph). In the world championship, races are held around the world.

24-hour race

One very famous car race takes place in Le Mans, France. Cars race around the circuit there for the whole 24 hours of a day! Each car has a team of three drivers who share the driving.

Aerodynamics

Designers of F1 and Le Mans cars build their cars to run as fast as possible. An **aerodynamic** car is key. Body parts, such as the wings and nose are all designed so that the air flows smoothly over them. This stops the air from slowing the car down.

Air flow

Air flow

Air flow

Off-roaders

Some vehicles are designed to be driven off the road. Off-road cars are used for work, such as farming, but are driven for fun, too.

Four-wheel drive

To climb up steep, rocky slopes and travel through rivers and mud, off-roaders need the power of **four-wheel drive**. This means all four wheels receive power from the engine. On a normal family car only two of the wheels are powered.

Tyres

The huge tyres on an off-road car make rough ground no problem. The deep **tread** on the wheels gives the vehicle good grip.

Hummer

The Hummer H1 is one of the most famous off-road vehicles. It can drive in 76 cm of water. A snorkel feeds air into the engine when it is underwater.

Rally cars

Rallying is a type of off-road motor racing. Cars race against the clock. They try and complete the course, or stage, in the fastest time.

Courses can be on all surfaces. Cars race on tarmac roads, gravel tracks and even snow and ice.
A driver's technique is to slide round the corners.

Suspension

In rallying, cars fly over the bumpy ground. The cars need excellent **suspension**. A set of springs connects the vehicle to the wheels. The springs soak up the bumps.

Across the desert

A long-distance rally race takes place every year. The first ever in 1979 ran in stages from France all the way to West Africa! Large parts of the course run through the desert.

City cars

Some people drive mainly in the city, or usually only make short journeys. They like to drive smaller cars. These cars are not very powerful, but they use less fuel and are cheap to run.

Smaller cars are also easier to **manoeuvre**. The Smart car (above) is so tiny it can park at the side of the road with its nose or rear to the kerb.

Power steering

Today, most cars have power steering. An **electric motor** is often used to power the steering wheel. This helps the driver turn the wheels, especially in tight spaces.

Electric cars

Burning fuel in cars is expensive and the exhaust fumes cause **pollution**. An electric car is less powerful but cleaner. In future you will see more of these vehicles. Instead of an engine, power comes from an on-board **battery** pack.

Luxury cars

Luxury cars are larger than normal family cars. They are extremely comfortable and have extra equipment.

The Rolls Royce Phantom (below) has rear-seat tables, a DVD entertainment system and a fridge in the back.

Armoured cars

The President of the United States has a very special luxury car. It is heavily armoured and nicknamed 'The Beast'. The glass is bulletproof and the car can run at 50 mph (80 kph) even with flat tyres.

Brakes

The heavier the car the harder you need to brake. Stepping on the brake pedal sends a fluid through pipes to each wheel. The fluid pushes brake pads against the wheels, making the car slow down.

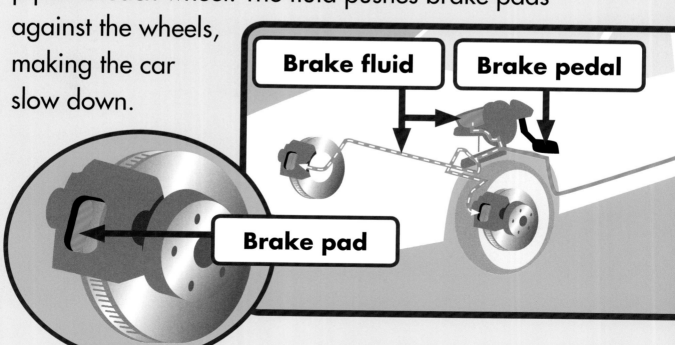

Brake fluid

Brake pedal

Brake pad

Custom cars

People often customise, or change, their cars to make them completely different from anything else. They want their vehicles to stand out from the crowd.

Hotrods

Hotrods are cars that have been altered to make them powerful and fast. Parts of the bodywork are chopped out or replaced to make them lighter, and a bigger engine is put in.

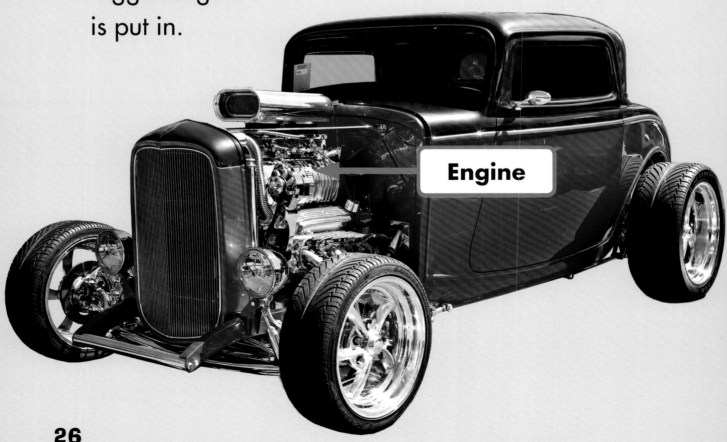

Engine

Many custom cars have a flashy paint job. Some cars have shiny **chrome** parts added.

Stretch Limos

Stretch limos are huge and luxurious customised cars. The front and back of the car are pulled apart and an extra section is put in the middle. They are hired out for special occasions and parties.

Dragsters

Dragsters are some of the fastest vehicles on Earth. With their deafening engines, they scream up to 330 mph (530 kph) in a matter of seconds.

Dragsters race against each other on a straight line called a drag strip. The race can be all over in five seconds!

Wheelie bar: This stops the car flipping into the air at high speeds.

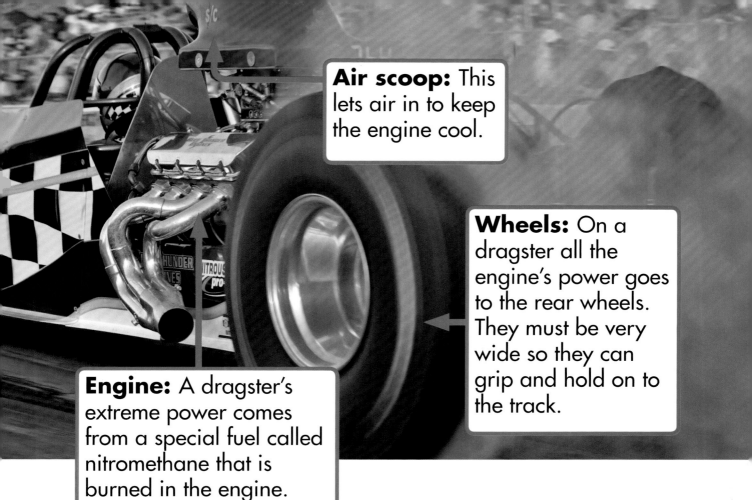

Air scoop: This lets air in to keep the engine cool.

Wheels: On a dragster all the engine's power goes to the rear wheels. They must be very wide so they can grip and hold on to the track.

Engine: A dragster's extreme power comes from a special fuel called nitromethane that is burned in the engine.

Land-speed record

The fastest a car has ever gone on land was in 1997. The jet-powered Thrust SSC raced at 763 mph (1,228 kph).

Glossary

aerodynamic designed to move through air easily and quickly

battery a container storing chemicals, which produces electrical power

biofuel a fuel made from living things such as plants

cabin the area for passengers in a vehicle such as a car

carbon fibre material made from threads of carbon used to make a car's bodywork strong but light

chrome a shiny, protective coating made from the metal chromium

convertible a car with a fold-down roof

diesel a heavy fuel used in diesel engines in cars and other vehicles

electric motor a machine powered by electricity that supplies power to moving parts

four-wheel drive a system which provides power to all four wheels of a vehicle

hatchback a family car, with a boot that opens like a door, but upwards

manoeuvre move something into position

pollution damage to the air with dirty and poisonous substances

radiator a sheet of thin tubes at the front of a car. They take hot water from the engine and cool it in the surrounding air.

saloon a family car with a closed boot separated from the passengers' seats

snorkel a tube that takes in air while you are underwater

suspension a system of springs between the wheels and a car to help the vehicle soak up bumps

tread the ridges on a tyre to prevent slipping

Index

Websites

www.shelbysupercars.com
Home of the world's fastest supercar.

www.diseno-art.com/encyclopedia/concept_cars/concept_cars.html
Have a look at these cars of the future.

http://auto.howstuffworks.com/car.htm
Find out how different parts of a car work.

DUDLEY SCHOOLS LIBRARY
AND INFORMATION SERVICE

BIG
MACHINES

Cranes

David and Penny Glover

W
FRANKLIN WATTS
LONDON•SYDNEY

Schools Library and Information Services

S00000674315

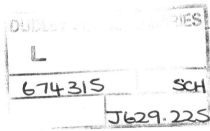

First published in 2004 by Franklin Watts
96 Leonard Street, London EC2A 4XD

Franklin Watts Australia
45-51 Huntley Street
Alexandria, NSW 2015

© Franklin Watts 2004

Series editor: Sarah Peutrill
Designer: Richard Langford
Art director: Jonathan Hair
Reading consultant: Margaret Perkins, Institute of Education, University of Reading

Picture credits: Colin Beere/Topham: 7b. Ian Britton/Freefoto: 23. David Frazier/Image
Works/Topham: 21b. Tiffany M Hermon/Image Works/Topham: 19. Image
Works/Topham: 8t, 17t. PA/Topham: 9, 15. Picturepoint/Topham: front cover, 6, 13t, 20.
Joel W. Rogers/Corbis: 22. Joe Sohm/Image Works/Topham: 21t. Courtesy of Street
Crane Co Ltd: 7t, 8b, 12, 14. Courtesy of Terex Cranes Ltd: 13b, 18.

With particular thanks to Street Crane and Terex for permission to use their photos.

Every attempt has been made to clear copyright. Should there be any inadvertent
omission, please apply to the publisher for rectification.

A CIP catalogue record for this book is available from the British Library.

ISBN 0 7496 5560 7

Printed in Malaysia